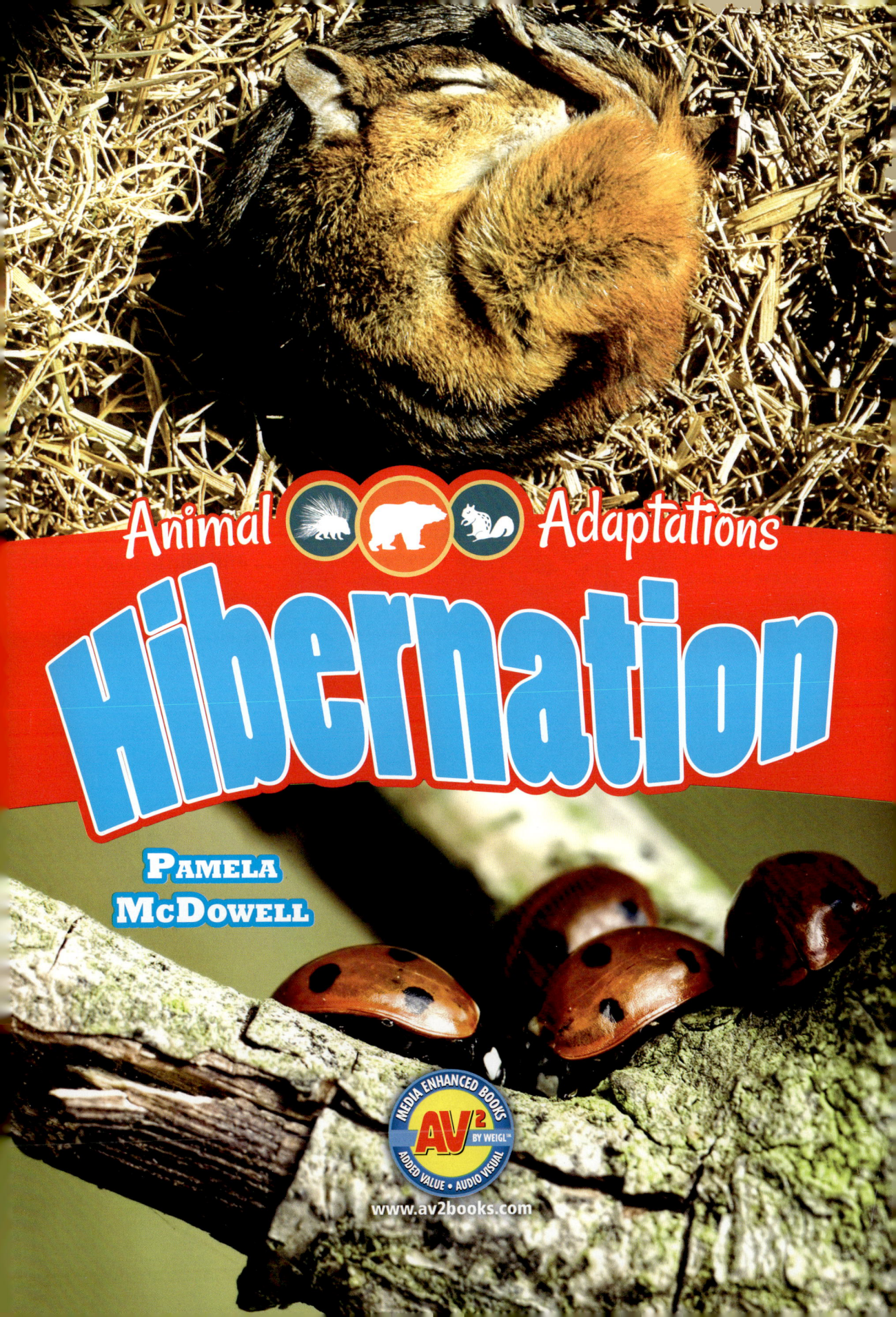

Animal Adaptations
Hibernation

Pamela McDowell

AV² provides enriched content that supplements and complements this book. Weigl's AV² books strive to create inspired learning and engage young minds in a total learning experience.

Your AV² Media Enhanced books come alive with...

 **Audio** Listen to sections of the book read aloud.

 **Key Words** Study vocabulary, and complete a matching word activity.

 **Video** Watch informative video clips.

 **Quizzes** Test your knowledge.

 **Embedded Weblinks** Gain additional information for research.

 **Slide Show** View images and captions, and prepare a presentation.

 **Try This!** Complete activities and hands-on experiments.

... and much, much more!

Go to www.av2books.com, and enter this book's unique code.

BOOK CODE

E649888

AV² by Weigl brings you media enhanced books that support active learning.

Published by AV2 by Weigl
350 5th Avenue, 59th Floor
New York, NY 10118
Website: www.av2books.com

Copyright ©2016 AV2 by Weigl
All rights reserved. No part of this publication may be reproduced, stored in a retrieval system, or transmitted in any form or by any means, electronic, mechanical, photocopying, recording, or otherwise, without the prior written permission of the publisher.

Library of Congress Cataloging-in-Publication Data

McDowell, Pamela.
  Hibernation / Pamela McDowell.
     pages cm. -- (Animal adaptations)
  Includes bibliographical references and index.
  ISBN 978-1-4896-3675-1 (hard cover : alk. paper) -- ISBN 978-1-4896-3676-8 (soft cover : alk. paper) -- ISBN 978-1-4896-3677-5 (single user ebkook) -- ISBN 978-1-4896-3678-2 (multi-user ebook)
  1. Hibernation--Juvenile literature. I. Title.
  QL755.M33 2015
  591.56'5--dc23
                                          2015000831

Printed in the United States of America in Brainerd, Minnesota
1 2 3 4 5 6 7 8 9   19 18 17 16 15

052015
WEP051515

Project Coordinator Aaron Carr
Art Director Terry Paulhus

Every reasonable effort has been made to trace ownership and to obtain permission to reprint copyright material. The publishers would be pleased to have any errors or omissions brought to their attention so that they may be corrected in subsequent printings.

Photo Credits
Weigl acknowledges Getty Images as its primary photo supplier for this title.
Page 16, courtesy of J.M. Storey, Carleton University.

Contents

AV[2] Book Code 2

What Is an Adaptation? 4

What Is Hibernation? 6

How Do Animals
Use Hibernation? 8

Types of Hibernation 10

How Does It Work? 12

Timeline 14

How Humans
Use Hibernation 16

Hibernation and Biodiversity 18

Conservation 20

Activity 21

Quiz 22

Key Words/Index 23

Log on to www.av2books.com 24

Animal Adaptations 3

What Is an Adaptation?

Animals have special features that help them survive in their natural **habitats**. These features are changes that have taken place over thousands, or even millions, of years. They are called adaptations. Animals that have adapted to their environment are able to survive for many **generations**. The adaptation will be passed on, and the **species** will grow stronger.

Every environment goes through changes that affect the plants and animals that live there. Extreme heat, cold, **drought**, or rainfall can make life difficult for a species. This is when animals need to adapt, or they may die. An adaptation may be one that helps an animal to survive on less water or to blend into its surroundings. Some animals have adapted to survive harsh weather by entering a state of deep sleep called hibernation.

During their months of hibernation, marmots use all their energy reserves. When they come out of their dens in spring, they are very hungry.

3 AMAZING HIBERNATION ADAPTATIONS

These animals have adapted different ways of protecting themselves in a harsh habitat.

Snails

In areas where there is little rainfall, snails can hibernate for more than two years.

Poorwill

Poorwill are the only birds that truly hibernate. They do so because their diet of insects is scarce during winter. During hibernation, a poorwill's body temperature drops to within 2° Fahrenheit (1° Celsius) of the air around it.

Hedgehog

A hedgehog will hibernate during winter and **estivate** during extreme heat.

What Is Hibernation?

Hibernation is a period of **dormancy**. It is like a very deep sleep. An animal that is hibernating may look as if it is dead. Its body temperature drops, its heartbeat slows down, and it takes only a few breaths each minute. These changes help it to save energy.

Animals that are dormant use very little energy. They get the energy they do need from stored body fat. Many dormant animals do not eat, drink, or move about at all. It can be very difficult to wake them. Animals that are unable to store enough body fat to last through a long hibernation wake sometimes to eat a little.

COLD CLIMATE

When winter approaches, some animals find a burrow and build a nest to prepare for hibernation. The Arctic ground squirrel **insulates** its nest with grass and hair. It spends so many months a year hibernating that the total time can add up to half its life.

HOT CLIMATE

Some animals escape heat and drought by estivating. They seek out cool, moist areas deep under the ground. The Australian desert spadefoot toad can estivate under the sand for up to three years, coming out only when it rains.

HOW THE AMERICAN BLACK BEAR HIBERNATES

American black bears live in forests and mountains in northern Mexico, the United States, and Canada. The bears hibernate during winter. Black bears that live in the far north or high in mountains have adapted to the extreme cold of those regions. They go into hibernation earlier in winter than bears that live farther south or at lower **altitudes**.

In milder climates, where the winters are not too harsh, black bears do not go into hibernation until November or December. These bears may hibernate for fewer than five months. They get to spend all of summer and most of fall building up their body fat.

In areas where winters are long and food is scarce, black bears go into hibernation in September or October. They need to build up their body fat through summer so they have enough energy for a hibernation that can last for six to seven months.

Shorter Hibernation

Longer Hibernation

Animal Adaptations 7

How Do Animals Use Hibernation?

The habitat in which an animal lives affects when and for how long it hibernates. An animal's hibernation cycle is adapted to suit the conditions of its habitat. Some animals hibernate for just hours while others hibernate, or estivate, for a year or more. The most common hibernation is for a season, usually winter.

The Andean hillstar hummingbird has a daily hibernation cycle. This tiny bird lives at a high altitude, where each night is like winter. During the day, the temperature is about 75°F (24°C). At night, it drops to about 14°F (–10°C). The Andean hillstar chooses a sheltered resting place that faces east, so it will be warmed by the rising Sun. It then survives the cold of the night by slowing its body systems and reducing its body temperature.

Every day, the Andean hillstar eats twice its body weight in food. It hibernates at night to save energy.

Hibernation and a Food Chain

Queen bumblebee, which are **primary consumers**, avoid cold weather by hibernating in soil or a tree stump. Bats are **secondary consumers**. Many species of bats hibernate when their diet of insects, small birds, and mice is scarce during cold months. Like other reptiles, rattlesnakes rely on the Sun for warmth. These **tertiary consumers** avoid cold and starvation by hibernating through winter. They awaken when the days are warmer and their prey is plentiful again.

Animal Adaptations 9

Types of Hibernation

Animals have adapted four different types of hibernation to survive winter. These are true hibernation, diapause, brumation, and shallow hibernation. Often the word hibernation is used to describe any kind of dormancy, but these specific terms are more correct. The term scientists use to describe hibernation depends upon the species.

Many **mammals**, reptiles, **amphibians**, insects, and birds have adapted dormancy to suit their habitats. Among mammals, only three groups are considered to be true hibernators. They are bats, marmots and ground squirrels, and hedgehogs.

Some species of bats migrate to avoid cold weather. Other species hibernate in caves or small protected spaces.

4 AMAZING TYPES OF HIBERNATION

True Hibernation

In true hibernation, an animal is close to death. Its body temperature drops to about 32°F (0°C). Its heart and breathing almost stop. A woodchuck's heart rate will drop from 153 beats a minute to 68 beats a minute when it enters hibernation.

Diapause

Diapause is when insects are dormant. Insects may enter diapause at any stage of their life cycle. Some butterflies survive winter by taking shelter in bushes. They become completely covered by snow. They can survive for three or four months in this condition.

Brumation

In the state of brumation, a reptile or an amphibian may appear to be frozen solid. Ice crystals can form in and on painted turtles. This state would kill a mammal. Natural antifreeze in the turtle's blood protects its tissues until the turtle thaws.

Shallow Hibernation

Bears are shallow hibernators. They slow down their body systems as other hibernators do, but the insulation of their fur keeps them warm. Bears can awaken quickly if danger approaches.

Animal Adaptations 11

How Does It Work?

Cooler days, less sunlight, and **hormones** may prompt an animal to prepare for hibernation. Some animals, such as bears, feed constantly in summer and early fall to build up body fat. This is the energy the animal's body will use during hibernation. Although an animal uses less energy while hibernating than it would if it was active, it will still lose body weight. A bear may still lose 40 percent of its body weight during hibernation.

Some animals gather and store food as winter approaches. Smaller animals, such as chipmunks, cannot store enough energy in their bodies for the entire winter. They must wake from hibernation every few weeks to snack.

Warmth or sound will wake an animal from hibernation. Its heart rate will rise quickly. The temperature around its head and heart will warm first. An animal in deep hibernation takes longer to awaken than an animal in shallow hibernation.

A woodchuck eats all summer to build up enough fat for its winter hibernation.

 # FOUR WAYS TO PREPARE FOR HIBERNATION

Shallow Hibernation

A chipmunk wakes often from shallow hibernation to feed. If it has not stored enough food, it may go into a deeper hibernation.

Torpor

Some hummingbirds go into a short hibernation on cool nights. Their heart rate drops from about 500 beats per minute to fewer than 50 beats a minute. They slowly become active before the Sun rises.

Hibernation in Groups

Snakes hibernate in groups to share their body heat. A snake burrow is called a hibernaculum.

Hibernation Alone

Most bears hibernate alone. Females give birth during hibernation. A female usually lets the cubs share her den during hibernation the following year as well.

Timeline

Over millions of years, marmots have not only survived in an environment that is constantly changing. They have also spread across a large part of Earth. Marmots are **extant** today because they have adapted to their cold habitat. Their small, furry ears do not lose heat as large ears would. They have thick fur. However, their most important adaptation may be hibernation.

All marmots hibernate. They build up their body weight beforehand by eating high-energy plants, such as berries. Some marmots go into deep hibernation. Some marmots wake for short periods if the temperature is mild, even taking a walk outside their burrows.

Up to 20 marmots may hibernate together in one burrow. Their body warmth helps to keep the burrow warm.

MARMOT SURVIVAL

13 million years ago  Marmots live in North America.

2 million years ago  As an ice age begins, the marmot's habitat becomes colder. Food is not available in winter. Marmots adapt to hibernate. Hibernation helps them survive.

1 million years ago  Marmots now also live in the mountains of Europe and in parts of Russia, Siberia, and central Asia. They also live in the Himalayas.

Today  Marmots hibernate for four to eight months each winter. They use their body fat reserves for energy while they are dormant.

Animal Adaptations   15

How Humans Use Hibernation

Scientists are interested in animal hibernation. They believe it has many potential uses in medicine. Some types of frogs have natural a natural antifreeze. Scientists want to learn how this **cryoprotectant** protects the frog's tissues when the frog freezes solid during hibernation. Freezing destroys human tissue.

At present, donated organs must be transplanted within hours. If organs could be frozen and thawed without damage, it would completely change the process. Organs could be stored, and they could be shipped around the world.

In winter, some types of frogs freeze solid, and their hearts and breathing stop. They return to normal in spring.

When an animal is hibernating, its body temperature is so low that it is actually in a state of **hypothermia**. Hospitals sometimes use hypothermia when treating serious injuries. They lower the patient's temperature to slow the body's systems. However, the process is risky because dropping the body's temperature too much can cause the heart to stop. Warming the body back up can cause damage to the kidneys and other internal organs. More knowledge about hibernation could make this treatment safer for patients.

The United States military is studying how hibernation could improve the safe transportation of wounded soldiers. The National Aeronautics and Space Administration (NASA) is researching its use for space travel. Having astronauts sleeping during a long flight could reduce the cost of space travel.

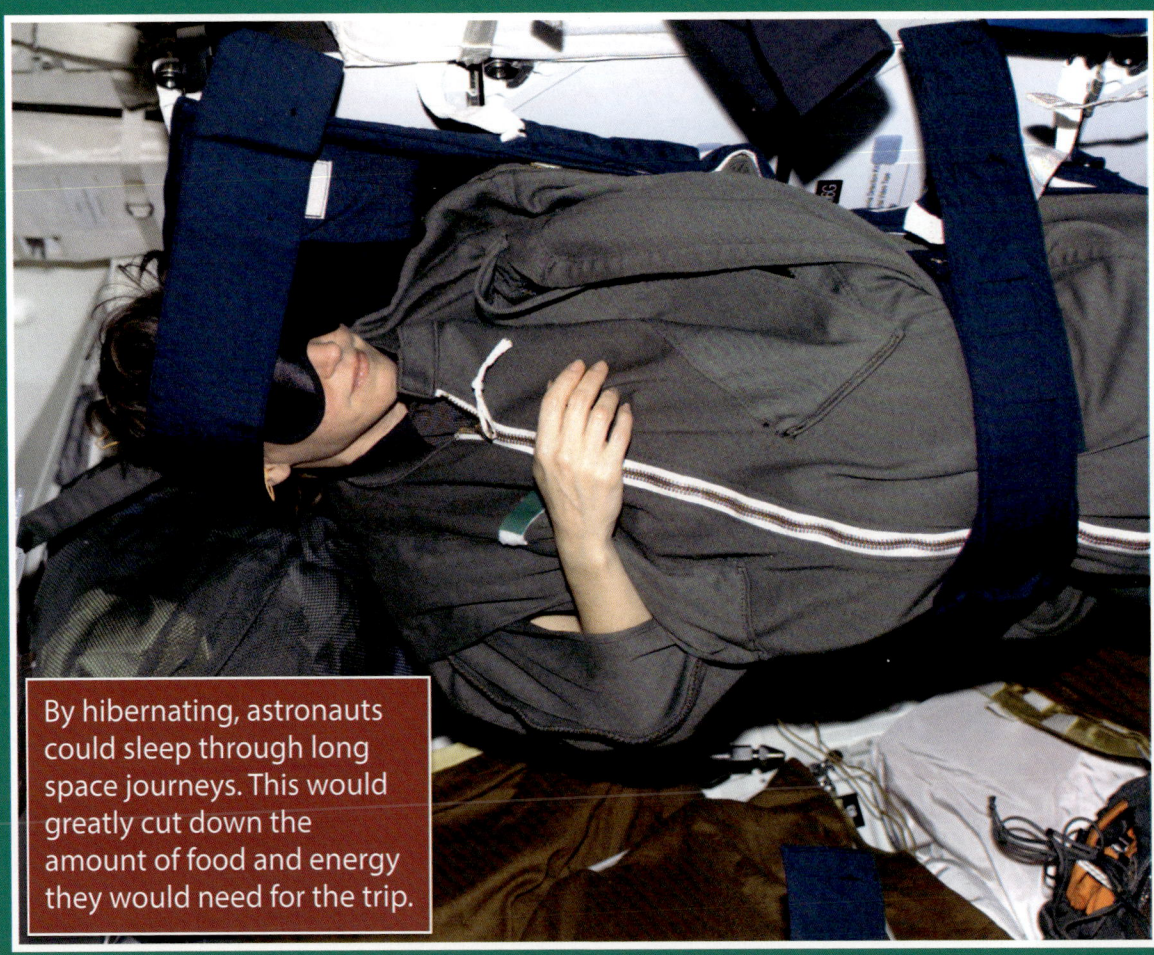

By hibernating, astronauts could sleep through long space journeys. This would greatly cut down the amount of food and energy they would need for the trip.

Animal Adaptations 17

Hibernation and Biodiversity

Biodiversity refers to the variety of plant and animal species in an **ecosystem**. Species rely on one another for survival. Greater biodiversity builds a healthier ecosystem by encouraging **natural selection**. The animals that have adapted best to the environment will survive and reproduce.

Ladybugs tend to hibernate in large groups, sometimes numbering thousands. Clustering together helps them to keep warm.

Hibernation is important to biodiversity. Animals that can survive extreme cold can expand their range into areas where other animals cannot live. When the animal awakens from hibernation, it will have less competition for food. The species grows stronger and the biodiversity of the area increases.

Hibernation can boost a species' survival, but it is dangerous for the individual animal. Deep hibernation is a balance between slowing body functions and death. Sometimes, animals do not survive. A harsh winter or poor preparation can be deadly. Waking from hibernation is also risky. More energy is needed to wake up than is used during several days of hibernation. An animal that awakens too often will use up its stored energy or food and starve before spring.

Hamsters may look as if they are dead when they hibernate for short periods.

Animal Adaptations

Conservation

Ecosystems are finely balanced. Change within one part of an environment, or within one species, can upset this balance and cause harm to other species. Destruction of the natural environment through logging, mining, and other development makes hibernation difficult. Species that hibernate need a habitat that provides natural places for burrows and dens.

When these areas are destroyed, animals cannot escape harsh winter conditions and may die. This upsets the balance within the ecosystem. Many organizations work to protect natural areas and the species within them. The World Wildlife Fund and the International Union for Conservation of Nature work to bring attention to issues of conservation.

Some bears dig a new den each year. Logging of trees can reduce the number of places where bears can make their dens.

Activity

Match each animal with the type of shelter it seeks for hibernation.

Answers: 1. D 2. B 3. A 4. C

Animal Adaptations 21

Quiz

Complete this quiz to test your knowledge of hibernation.

1 What is the name of the only bird that has adapted true hibernation?

A. Poorwill

2 Why do animals hibernate?

A. To survive extreme temperatures or food or water shortages.

3 Where does a queen bumblebee hibernate?

A. In soil or a tree stump

4 What animal is a shallow hibernator?

A. A bear

5 How much food does an Andean hillstar hummingbird eat each day?

A. Twice its body weight

6 Which mammals are true hibernators?

A. Bats, marmots, ground squirrels, and hedgehogs

7 What is biodiversity?

A. The variety of species of plant and animals in an ecosystem

8 How does land development affect hibernating animals?

A. There is no place for dens or burrows

9 What could wake an animal from hibernation?

A. Warmth or sound

10 What is diapause?

A. A period of dormancy for an insect

22 Hibernation

Key Words

altitudes: heights above sea level

amphibians: animals that live both on land and in water

cryoprotectant: substance that protects tissue from damage caused by freezing

dormancy: a state of being in a very deep sleep

drought: a long period without rain

ecosystem: all the living things that exist in a particular habitat

estivate: be dormant during hot weather

extant: still existing; not extinct

generations: relating to the normal life spans of animals

habitats: the natural environments of living things

hormones: chemical substances made by an animal's body that affect the way it develops and behaves

hypothermia: when a body's temperature drops below what is normally needed for its systems to function

insulates: uses materials to prevent the loss of heat

mammals: warm-blooded animals that feed milk to their young

natural selection: a process whereby animals that have better adapted to their environment survive and pass on those adaptations to their young

primary consumers: animals that feed on plants

secondary consumers: animals that feed on plant-eating animals

species: a group of plants or animals that are alike

tertiary consumers: animals that feed on other animals

Index

amphibians 10, 11
antifreeze 11, 16
Asia 15
astronauts 17

bats 9, 10, 21
bears 7, 11, 12, 13, 20, 21, 22
birds 5, 8, 9, 10, 13, 22
body fat 6, 7, 12, 15
brumation 10, 11
bumblebees 9, 22
burrows 6, 13, 14, 20, 22
butterflies 11, 21

Canada 7
chipmunks 12, 13
cryoprotectants 16

diapause 10, 11, 22
dormancy 5, 6, 10, 11, 15, 22

estivation 5, 6, 8
Europe 15

frogs 16

ground squirrels 6, 10, 22

habitats 4, 5, 8, 10, 14, 15, 20
hamsters 19
hedgehogs 5, 10, 22
Himalayas 15
hormones 12
hummingbirds 8, 13, 22
hypothermia 17

ice age 15
insects 5, 9, 10, 11, 22
International Union for Conservation of Nature 20

ladybugs 18

mammals 10, 11, 22
marmots 4, 10, 14, 15, 22
Mexico 7

National Aeronautics and Space Administration (NASA) 17
nest 6
North America 5

poorwills 5, 22
primary consumers 9

reptiles 9, 10, 11
Russia 15

secondary consumers 9
shallow hibernators 10, 11, 13, 22
Siberia 15
snails 5
snakes 9, 13

tertiary consumers 9
toads 6, 21
true hibernation 10, 11, 22
turtles 11

United States 7, 17

weight 8, 12, 14, 22
woodchucks 11, 12
World Wildlife Fund 20

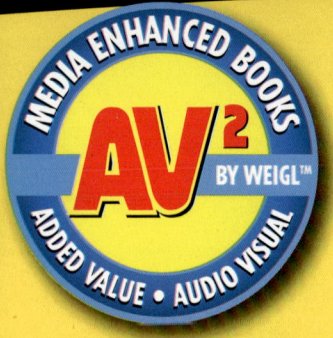

Log on to www.av2books.com

AV² by Weigl brings you media enhanced books that support active learning. Go to www.av2books.com, and enter the special code found on page 2 of this book. You will gain access to enriched and enhanced content that supplements and complements this book. Content includes video, audio, weblinks, quizzes, a slide show, and activities.

AV² Online Navigation

Audio
Listen to sections of the book read aloud.

Book Pages
AV² pages directly correspond to pages in the book.

Video
Watch informative video clips.

Key Words
Study vocabulary, and complete a matching word activity.

Embedded Weblinks
Gain additional information for research.

Quizzes
Test your knowledge.

Slide Show
View images and captions, and prepare a presentation.

Try This!
Complete activities and hands-on experiments.

AV² was built to bridge the gap between print and digital. We encourage you to tell us what you like and what you want to see in the future.

Sign up to be an AV² Ambassador at www.av2books.com/ambassador.

Due to the dynamic nature of the internet, some of the URLs and activities provided as part of AV² by Weigl may have changed or ceased to exist. AV² by Weigl accepts no responsibility for any such changes. All media enhanced books are regularly monitored to update addresses and sites in a timely manner. Contact AV² by Weigl at 1-866-649-3445 or av2books@weigl.com with any questions, comments, or feedback.